NHL HOT STREAKS

BY RYAN WILLIAMSON

MOMENTUM

Published by The Child's World®
1980 Lookout Drive • Mankato, MN 56003-1705
800-599-READ • www.childsworld.com

Photographs ©: Jerome Davis/Icon Sportswire/AP
Images, cover, 1; David Berding/Icon Sportswire/
AP Images, 5; A. E. Maloof/AP Images, 6; AP
Images, 8; Steve Babineau/National Hockey
League/Getty Images, 10; Gene Puskar/AP
Images, 13; Doug Griffin/Toronto Star/Getty
Images, 14; Fred Jewell/AP Images, 17; Kathy
Willens/AP Images, 18; Frank Franklin II/AP
Images, 20; Steven Kingsman/Icon Sportswire/AP
Images, 22, 25; John Crouch/Cal Sport Media/AP
Images, 26; Red Line Editorial, 28

ISBN 9781503832305
LCCN 2018963088

Printed in the United States of America
PA02422

ABOUT THE AUTHOR

Ryan Williamson is a sportswriter based in the Minneapolis–Saint Paul area. He has written articles that have appeared in various publications across the country. He graduated from the University of Missouri with a degree in print/digital sports journalism.

CONTENTS

MOMENTUM

FAST FACTS

Game Rules

▶ In a National Hockey League (NHL) game, each team has six skaters on the ice. There are three forwards, two defensemen, and a goalie.

▶ When a penalty is called in hockey, the player must sit in the penalty box for two or five minutes. His team is then short one player for however long the penalty lasts.

The NHL Is Born

▶ The NHL officially began in 1917. Two teams remain from that first season. They are the Montreal Canadiens and Toronto Maple Leafs (called the Arenas at the time).

The Stanley Cup

▶ The NHL regular season is 82 games long. The eight teams with the most points in the Eastern and Western **Conferences** make the playoffs. Then, each conference has an eight-team tournament. Each round is made up of a best-of-seven series. The winner of each conference meets in the Stanley Cup Final. The winner gets the Stanley Cup.

Hockey is a fast-paced game. ▶

CHAPTER ONE

ORR'S FANTASTIC FINISH

Bobby Orr of the Boston Bruins skated quickly toward the goal. He looked to his teammate who had the puck. The Bruins were in a tight game against the St. Louis Blues in the 1970 Stanley Cup Final. Orr had been red hot all season. Though he was a defenseman, Orr had led the league with 120 points. He already had eight goals and 11 assists in the playoffs. Now he wanted one more.

With the game in overtime, Orr and the Bruins needed just one goal to win. With that in mind, Orr was trying to get to the net. He wanted to be close when the pass came to him. This strategy had worked throughout the playoffs. If the pass came right to Orr's stick, he could quickly flick the puck into the net.

◄ **Bobby Orr (left) celebrates his game-winning goal.**

▲ Orr won four major awards in 1969-70.

Orr's teammate waited for a few seconds. Then Orr appeared in front of the net. The pass came directly to him. There was a small open space. Orr shot the puck into it. Just then, he was tripped and flew through the air. He raised his arms in triumph as he did. Orr knew his goal had won Boston the Stanley Cup championship.

Following the game, Orr celebrated in the locker room with his teammates. His smile was hard to miss. Orr received award after award for his success in the **postseason**. He had wrapped up one of the greatest individual seasons ever on a high note with a goal that left him and the Bruins flying high.

GERRY CHEEVERS' TRIUMPH

Fans wanted Boston to do well again during the 1971–72 season. And the Bruins did, thanks to goaltender Gerry Cheevers. He took matters into his own hands and helped the team to 32 straight games without a loss. Eight of those games finished in a tie. Undefeated streaks are hard to string together. In hockey, pucks bounce oddly and can squeeze by a goalie. That's what made Cheevers' run so special.

CHAPTER TWO

AN UNBEATEN STREAK

Boston Bruins fans walked into the arena. They wore the Bruins' colors of black and gold. They wanted their team to knock off the Philadelphia Flyers. The Bruins and Flyers had always been **rivals**. But this game in 1979 was tenser than usual. Philadelphia had a chance to go 29 games without losing. That would be a new NHL record.

The Bruins players thought they would be able to get Philadelphia off its game with lots of hitting and fighting. Bill Barber of the Flyers called the game a "mini-war."[1] In the first period, Boston took a penalty while already down 1–0. This was the Flyers' chance to extend their lead. Barber did just that on a long shot that raced passed Bruins goaltender Gilles Gilbert.

◄ **The Flyers and Bruins faced off in Boston Garden.**

Late in the game, Philadelphia led 5–2. The seconds ticked down, and Boston fans were leaving the building in large groups. When the buzzer went off, Philadelphia had officially set the record for 29 **consecutive** games without a loss.

"We had a great blend," Barber said. "We had some guys . . . that did a great job. . . . We had some of the older guys like myself, and [center Bobby Clarke], then we had the young guns there too that carried the load."[2]

The undefeated streak didn't end after beating Boston, either. Six games later, the Flyers still hadn't lost. They went into the Minnesota North Stars' arena, hoping to make it 36 games without a loss. This time, the amazing run finally came to an end. Flyers goalie Phil Myre was helpless as the North Stars shot seven pucks past him. Philadelphia lost 7–1.

The hot streak was over, but it had been an incredible run. Philadelphia had gone 86 days without a loss. The Flyers had won 25 games and tied ten. Eighteen different players scored at least one goal, with forward Reggie Leach netting 25. And all of that success helped prepare the Flyers to make a run to that year's Stanley Cup Final.

Bobby Clarke of the Flyers scored against the ▶ New York Rangers in the 1979 Stanley Cup playoffs.

CHAPTER THREE

GRETZKY'S RECORD GOALS

The referee raised his arm, signaling a penalty. Wayne Gretzky knew this was his time to make a difference. His Edmonton Oilers trailed the Philadelphia Flyers 1–0 on December 31, 1981, but now they would have a **power play**. The 20-year-old Gretzky knew he'd have more space on the ice to make a big play. And sure enough, he found it. Gretzky got in position near the Flyers' goal. His teammate, Paul Coffey, ripped a shot. The goalie saved it, but Gretzky was there to flick the puck into the net. Midway through the first period, the score was tied 1–1, and Gretzky's season-opening hot streak continued.

In some ways, Gretzky's entire career was a hot streak. He had amazing games and seasons, and even periods. Some of his records might never be broken. Yet his hottest stretch might have been his start to the 1981–82 season.

◄ **Wayne Gretzky celebrates a goal during his famous hot streak.**

Gretzky opened the season hot, scoring seven goals in the first 11 games. Then he started really heating up. After 30 games, he had scored 31 goals. That put him on pace to match the NHL record of 50 goals in 50 games. Montreal's Maurice "Rocket" Richard had set the standard in 1944–45, when seasons were 50 games.[3] The Islanders' Mike Bossy had matched that feat in 1980–81. He scored his 50th goal in his 50th game.

In his 38th game, Gretzky scored four more goals, bringing his total to 45. That left him 11 games to score five more goals. The young star didn't want to wait. He scored his second goal against the Flyers on a high **slapshot** midway through the first period. He sent another slapshot over the goalie's right shoulder in the second. In the third period, Gretzky picked up the puck at the blue line. He skated around a defender. Then he beat the goalie again, this time shooting over the goalie's glove. Now he was just one goal short of the record.

Trailing by one, the Flyers pulled their goalie. That meant they could add another skater to help them score. With time ticking down, Gretzky got the puck. He shot it into the empty net with three seconds left, giving the Oilers a 7–5 win. Gretzky had scored 50 goals in 39 games. "The Great One" went on to score 92 goals that season.[4] No one in hockey history to that point had scored more than 76. And no one since Gretzky has surpassed it.

▲ **Gretzky (right) battles for the puck.**

CHAPTER FOUR

THE KINGS' RUN

The seconds were slowly ticking down on the large, electronic scoreboard during Game 6 of the 2012 Stanley Cup Final. Both the Los Angeles Kings and New Jersey Devils skated around, waiting for the game to end. The Kings fans felt the same way as they waved their towels in celebration. The Kings led 6–1. Los Angeles had been a part of the NHL for decades. But in 2012, it was finally time for the Kings to win their first Stanley Cup.

It was a miracle that Los Angeles even got to the Stanley Cup Final that year. The Kings were the lowest ranked team in their conference going into the playoffs. Yet once in, they began dominating their opponents. Fans became more excited as the Kings **upset** one opponent after the other. This led them to Game 6 of the Stanley Cup Final. Fittingly, their red-hot playoff run ended with their best game yet.

◄ **Colin Fraser and Brad Richardson of the Kings celebrate Fraser's goal during the Stanley Cup Final.**

▲ **The Kings worked together to try and stop a Devils player from scoring.**

Early on, the Kings got good shots near the goal. Los Angeles fired shot after shot at Devils goalie Martin Brodeur. After around 11 minutes of trying, the Kings finally broke through. A Los Angeles defenseman sent a shot toward the net. Kings forward Dustin Brown saw the puck. He put his stick on it. With the **deflection**, Brodeur could not see the puck. It landed in the back of the net.

Brown continued his strong play. Minutes later, he had the puck again. He quickly turned toward the net and fired a hard shot. This time, his teammate Jeff Carter deflected the shot for a goal. The noise was deafening in the building as the Los Angeles fans celebrated. Los Angeles continued to score.

When the clock showed ten seconds left in the game, the entire arena cheered and counted down. When there was no time left, Los Angeles players began to celebrate. They all grouped together and hugged each other. Their unlikely playoff run had led them all the way to the championship. A few minutes later, the Kings were given the Stanley Cup.

JAKE GUENTZEL

Jake Guentzel had a playoff performance for the ages in 2017. He came in as a **rookie** and showed up as one of the Penguins' best scorers. In the playoffs, Guentzel had 21 points, which is tied for the most by any rookie in NHL postseason history. He scored important goals and was great at receiving passes from teammate Sidney Crosby and putting the puck in the net. Guentzel's play was key to Pittsburgh winning the Stanley Cup in 2017.

CHAPTER FIVE

A MAGNIFICENT DEBUT

The Toronto Maple Leafs followed Auston Matthews onto the ice for their season opener in October 2016. Their skates slid on top of the freshly smoothed surface. To Matthews, it was a comfortable and familiar feeling. Matthews was making his NHL **debut** that night in Ottawa, Canada, against the Ottawa Senators. Matthews had been the No. 1 overall draft pick, and people had high expectations for him. Fans from Toronto flocked to Ottawa to see what Matthews was capable of.

Matthews glided around the ice early in the game. At 19 years old, Matthews was skating quickly around experienced Senators defensemen. Nearly nine minutes into the game, Matthews was right in front of the net. His teammate passed him the puck. Matthews saw the Senators goalie lying down. There was a lot of open space in the net. Matthews flicked the puck in.

◄ **Auston Matthews was focused during his first NHL game against the Senators.**

Just after scoring, Matthews was tripped. He struggled to stay upright as he skated over to the boards to celebrate his first NHL goal. Matthews' teammates helped him regain his balance and hugged him while fans filled the stadium with yells of excitement. Matthews' parents hugged each other with tears rolling down their faces. It was a proud moment for them.

That was only the beginning. Minutes later, Matthews was able to skate quickly around defensemen and keep his eyes on the puck. His persistent play brought him to the net. And he once again fired the puck past Senators goaltender Craig Anderson.

BRIAN BOUCHER SHUTS THE DOOR

Over his 13 seasons in the NHL, Brian Boucher was a good goalie but never a superstar. However, one amazing stretch in 2003–04 will never be forgotten. It began on December 22 when Boucher gave up a second-period goal to the Nashville Predators. He didn't give up another until January 11, 2004. The Atlanta Thrashers scored in the first period to end Boucher's record shutout streak at 332:01. That meant he went 332 minutes and one second between giving up a goal. That included five full games in a row without giving up a goal, which was also a record.

▲ **Matthews sneaks the puck past the Ottawa goalie.**

Matthews scored two more goals that night. Each of Matthews' goals led to cheers from Toronto fans. Though the Maple Leafs ended up losing in overtime, there was plenty to celebrate. The Toronto crowd knew their highly regarded rookie had the chance to become a legend. Matthews was the first player to score four goals in his debut game in the NHL's modern era. The modern NHL era started in the 1943–44 season.

CHAPTER SIX

OVECHKIN FINALLY WINS THE CUP

Forward Alexander Ovechkin of the Washington Capitals stood at center ice, waiting for the puck to drop in Game 5 of the 2018 Stanley Cup Final. His gap-toothed smile was easy to see. Ovechkin had been a scoring machine in the 2018 playoffs. He came into the game with 14 goals and 12 assists.

The moment to shine for Ovechkin came in the second period. Washington's opponent, the Vegas Golden Knights, had just scored to tie the game at 1–1. The Vegas fans cheered loudly but soon became quiet when their team got a penalty.

The call on the Golden Knights meant the Capitals went on the power play. Over his career, Ovechkin had shown his ability to score goals. He skills became even harder to defend against on the power play.

◄ **Alexander Ovechkin held the Stanley Cup after the Capitals defeated the Golden Knights.**

A pass came to Ovechkin's stick, and he immediately fired the puck toward the net. The puck sneaked past the goaltender. Players hugged in celebration as Washington took a 2–1 lead. With his 15th goal, Ovechkin now had more than any other player in the playoffs.

The Capitals held a 4–3 lead late in the game. The clock continued to count down, and the Washington fans were getting more and more excited. Many had traveled to Las Vegas in hope of seeing the Capitals win their first-ever championship.

STANLEY CUP WINS

TEAM	WINS
Montreal Canadiens	23
Toronto Maple Leafs	13
Detroit Red Wings	11
Boston Bruins	6
Chicago Blackhawks	6
Edmonton Oilers	5
Pittsburgh Penguins	5
New York Rangers	4
New York Islanders	4

With less than one second remaining, Vegas had one more chance to tie the game. The Golden Knights had the puck near the Washington goal. They put a shot near the net. All the Capitals defenders watched goaltender Braden Holtby stop the shot. The clock had expired.

Ovechkin raced to celebrate with his teammates. His helmet, gloves, and stick were lying on the ground as he joined his teammates in a big mob on the ice. The players were hugging and screaming in delight. After that, Washington finally got to touch the Stanley Cup. Ovechkin grabbed the trophy, put it over his head, and let out a scream.

"I just wanted to do whatever I can to help win the Cup. And we did it," said Ovechkin.[5] He was a Stanley Cup champion, and his scoring was key in the Capitals winning the championship.

THINK ABOUT IT

► What characteristics do you think people on hockey teams need in order to win the Stanley Cup? Explain your answer.
► How do you think athletes are able to perform well under intense pressure?
► If you were on a sports team, do you think it would be important to support your teammates? Why or why not?

GLOSSARY

conferences (KAHN-fur-uhn-sez): Conferences are groups of teams. The NHL has Eastern and Western Conferences.

consecutive (kuhn-SEK-yuh-tiv): Consecutive means it happened in a row. The Philadelphia Flyers went 35 consecutive games without a loss.

debut (day-BYOO): A debut is the first time someone appears in their current role. Matthews made his NHL debut in October 2016.

deflection (di-FLEK-shun): Deflection means to change the direction of something. The deflection allowed the hockey player to score.

postseason (POST-see-zun): The postseason is a series of games played after the regular season that decides a champion. Orr had a successful postseason.

power play (POW-ur PLAY): A power play is when one team briefly has more players on the rink because the other team committed a penalty. Gretzky scored on a power play.

rivals (RY-vuhls): Rivals are teams that have an especially intense history against each other. The Bruins and Flyers are rivals.

rookie (ROOK-ee): A rookie is a first-year player. Matthews was a rookie in 2016.

slapshot (SLAP-shot): A slapshot is when a hockey player powerfully swings his or her stick and then hits the puck. Gretzky made a slapshot.

upset (uhp-SET): Upset means to defeat unexpectedly. The Kings upset teams in the playoffs.

SOURCE NOTES

1. Adam Kimelman. "Flyers' 35-Game Undefeated Streak Stokes Memories." *NHL*. NHL, 28 Oct. 2017. Web. 29 Jan. 2019.

2. Ibid.

3. "Gretzky Shatters 50-Goal Record." *New York Times*. New York Times Company, 31 Dec. 1981. Web. 29 Jan. 2019.

4. "99 Reasons Why Wayne Gretzky Is 'The Great One.'" *NHL*. NHL, 2 Oct. 2004. Web. 29 Jan. 2019.

5. Greg Wyshynski. "The 'But' Stops Here: Alex Ovechkin's 14-Year Stanley Cup Chase Is Over." *ESPN*. ESPN Internet Ventures, 8 June 2018. Web. 29 Jan. 2019.

TO LEARN MORE

BOOKS

Herman, Gail. *Who Is Wayne Gretzky?*
New York, NY: Grosset & Dunlap, 2015.

Mikoley, Kate. *Hockey: Stats, Facts, and Figures.*
New York, NY: Gareth Stevens Publishing, 2018.

Page, Sam. *Hockey: Then to Wow!* New York, NY: Liberty Street, 2017.

WEBSITES

Visit our website for links about the NHL: **childsworld.com/links**

Note to Parents, Teachers, and Librarians: We routinely verify our Web links to make sure they are safe and active sites. So encourage your readers to check them out!